Light

Cody Crane

Content Consultant
Elizabeth Case DeSantis, M.A. Elementary Education
Julia A. Stark Elementary School, Stamford, Connecticut

Reading Consultant
Jeanne M. Clidas, Ph.D.
Reading Specialist

Children's Press®
An Imprint of Scholastic Inc.

Library of Congress Cataloging-in-Publication Data
Names: Crane, Cody, author.
Title: Light/by Cody Crane.
Other titles: Rookie read-about science.
Description: New York: Children's Press, an imprint of Scholastic Inc.,
[2019] | Series: Rookie read-about science
Identifiers: LCCN 2018027647| ISBN 9780531134085 (library
binding) | ISBN 9780531138021 (pbk.)
Subjects: LCSH: Light—Juvenile literature.
Classification: LCC QC360 .C72285 2019 | DDC 535—dc23

Produced by Spooky Cheetah Press
Design: Brenda Jackson
Digital Imaging: Bianca Alexis
Creative Direction: Judith E. Christ for Scholastic Inc.
© 2019 by Scholastic Inc. All rights reserved.

Published in 2019 by Children's Press, an imprint of
Scholastic Inc.

Printed in Heshan, China 62

SCHOLASTIC, CHILDREN'S PRESS, ROOKIE READ-ABOUT®,
and associated logos are trademarks and/or registered
trademarks of Scholastic Inc., 557 Broadway, New York,
NY 10012.

1 2 3 4 5 6 7 8 9 10 R 28 27 26 25 24 23 22 21 20 19

Scholastic Inc., 557 Broadway, New York,
NY 10012

Photographs ©: Javier Brosch/Shutterstock; back cover:
martin-dm/iStockphoto; 2-3: plusphoto/iStockphoto; 5:
Squaredpixels/iStockphoto; 7: Blend Images/KidStock/
Getty Images; 9: Allexander/Dreamstime; 10: tatyana_
tomsickova/iStockphoto; 13: Sunny studio/Shutterstock;
15: Tappasan Phurisamrit/Shutterstock, Inc.; 17: Claus
Lunau/Science Photo Library/Getty Images; 19: Topic Photo
Agency/age fotostock; 21: Theo Allofs/Minden Pictures;
22: martin-dm/iStockphoto; 25: Schrempp Erich/Science
Source/Getty Images; 27: Mike Pellinni/Shutterstock; 28
colored paper: Svetamart/Dreamstime; 28 straws: Slavica
Stajic/Shutterstock; 28 tape: Carolyn Franks/Dreamstime;
29 center right: Lol Johnson/DK Images; 29 top left:
Andy Crawford/DK Images; 29 top right: Lol Johnson/
DK Images; 29 bottom right: Lol Johnson/DK Images;
30 top: Sunny studio/Shutterstock; 30 center: Tappasan
Phurisamrit/Shutterstock, Inc.; 30 bottom: Squaredpixels/
iStockphoto; 31 top: Mike Pellinni/Shutterstock; 31 center:
martin-dm/iStockphoto; 31 bottom: Theo Allofs/Minden
Pictures; 32: PhotographyByMK/Shutterstock.

Table of Contents

Chapter 1

Let It Shine

Light allows you to see the world around you. These kids would not be able to read their books without light.

The sun gives off a lot of light. It makes Earth bright during the day.

How can the sun's bright light affect your skin in summer?

Sunlight warms Earth's surface and makes life possible. Plants, like these sunflowers, need light to grow.

Why do you think these flowers are called sunflowers?

Chapter 2

Seeing in the Dark

It gets dark when the sun sets. You need another type of light to be able to see.

What types of light can help you see at night?

People switch on lightbulbs
when they need extra light.
The lightbulbs run on **electricity**.
Electricity powers lightbulbs
so they glow.

Where
might you
find electric
lights?

13

People at a festival send paper **lanterns** into the air. A flame from a candle causes the lanterns to glow. Things that are really hot, like fire, give off light.

What other hot things, like these lanterns, give off light?

Chapter 3

On the Move

Light can move from place to place. The sun is very far away. Its light must travel millions of miles to reach Earth, our planet.

Would light and heat from the sun take longer to reach planets beyond Earth?

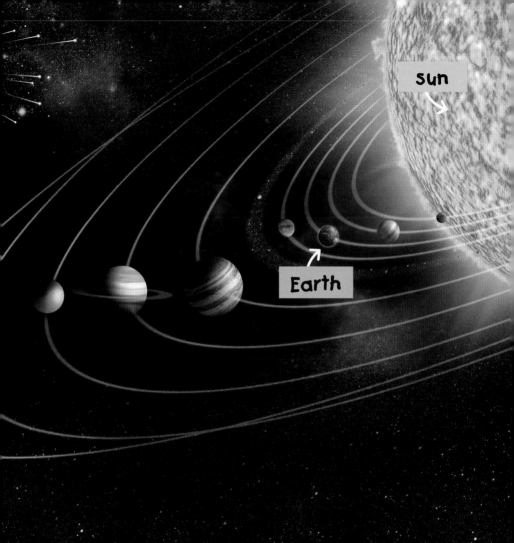

Sun

Earth

Light moves in a straight line.
Try shining a flashlight at something.
A spot of light will appear
straight ahead.

What
would
happen if you
moved your hand
in front of a
flashlight's
beam?

18

Some things block light.
A **shadow** forms on the other side
of the object. That is an area where
light cannot reach.

What is
interesting
about the
zebras'
shadows?

21

Chapter 4

Bending Light

Light can **reflect** off some things.
It bounces off shiny surfaces.
That is why you can see your reflection
in a mirror.

Where else could this duckling see its reflection?

Light bends as it passes through some objects. A glass filled with water bends light. That is why the straw looks crooked when seen above and below the water.

Have you ever seen this happen?

25

Light looks white. But it is made up of many colors. Light splits into separate colors when it passes through water drops. That makes a **rainbow**.

When do you think you would see a rainbow in the sky?

How else does light change the world around you?

27

Playing with Shadows

Can you create a shadow puppet?

Remember to ask an adult for help with this activity.

1. You will need some paper and scissors, straws, and tape.

28

2. Cut animal shapes from the paper. Stick a straw on the back with tape.

3. Hold the cutout in front of a wall and use a lamp or flashlight to shine a light on it.

What Happened?

Your cutout blocks the light shining on it. That creates a shadow on the wall. You can use your hands to make shadow animals, too!

electricity (ih-lek-TRIH-suh-tee): a type of power created by moving, charged particles

- *Lightbulbs are powered by* **electricity**.

lanterns (lan-turnz): light sources, like candles, held inside a see-through case

- **Lanterns** *help people see in the dark.*

light (lite): thing that allows you to see

- *People need* **light** *to be able to read books.*

rainbow (rayn-boh): an arc made up of bands of color

- *Sun shining through water droplets creates a* **rainbow** *in the sky.*

reflect (ri-flekt): to bounce off a surface

- *Light* **reflects** *off shiny objects, like a mirror.*

shadow (shad-oh): a dark area formed when an object blocks light

- *When an object blocks sunlight, it casts a* **shadow**.

Index

Facts for N

Visit this
Scholastic website for
more information on light,
and to download
the Reader's
Guide for this series:
**http://www.factsfornow.
scholastic.com**
Enter the keyword
Light

About the Author

Cody Crane
is an award-winning
children's science
writer. She lives in Texas
with her husband
and son.